Pockets & Panties

Canise Gray

Copyright © 2015 Christina Marie

All rights reserved.

ISBN: 069262161X
ISBN-13: 978-0692621615

To Lafayette, Caroline, Dartmouth, Parker, Ben, and Avant for making a way.

CONTENTS

	Acknowledgments	i
I.	Introduction	1
	The Concept	4
	Why You Need This Book	6
II	The Fine Print	7
	Definitions	8
	Rule 1: W.Y.S.I.W.Y.G.	10
	Rule 2: Women are Just Like Men	20
	Rule 3. All Women Want Money	29
III	The Paradigm	33
	Head	35
	Heart	48
	Pockets	64

ACKNOWLEDGMENTS

Thanks to everyone that provided inspiration and support. And, special thanks to my Mom.

I. INTRODUCTION

When I met him it was love at second sight. I always joked with him that he was deceptively attractive because I did not realize how attractive he was until we met for lunch more than a month later. We met at young professional's networking function and did the typical dance, exchanged business cards and said "we should keep in touch."

A month later when he finally contacted me I was already head over heels in love with someone else and almost declined his lunch invitation. I was not really in love of course. It was the kind of love women feel when we meet a man that has all the right credentials, features, and pedigree we desire. The other guy was an engineer that I had spent one unforgettable weekend with in Atlanta at a mutual friend's house. No there was no wild sex party going on. He was in town for a wedding and I was in town for a party. When we met, the chemistry was undeniable. He lived in California, I lived in DC, and thus, I spent the entire weekend trying to figure out how to make a long distance love affair work.

Upon my return to DC, I still contemplated "going the distance" with the other guy however such notions quickly disseminated after **one** lunch with him. He was a Commercial Banker with an MBA. His company email and voicemail verified that he was indeed who his business card purported him to be. Again… as in *Bridget Jones' Diary*, I heard wedding bells. I was approaching thirty and just knew that he was the one I had been waiting for to make my dreams of FINALLY being married come true.

Unlike the other guy, he was local. This major bonus would make courtship a breeze, or so I thought. It took me almost three years to realize that the wedding bells that played on repeat in my head had nothing to do with feelings of love for whatever guy I was fantasizing into my life at the time. The wedding bells had everything to do with me seeing a man as my *Cerise sur le gateau* (icing on the cake). Even by the toughest critic's standards I was accomplished, thus most capable of taking care of myself. Before thirty I was a licensed attorney, making well over six figures, drove a luxury car and lived in one of the most expensive areas in DC. By many standards, I had definitely "made it." Still, I spent most of my time looking for, pining over, or fantasizing about a man to "make my life complete."

Only after trying and failing at every trick in my book (and even a few of my girlfriends books) to snag him did I begin to evaluate why I did what I did and why women have a book of tricks to snag a man. This curiosity led to heated, and often painful battles about "us" or the lack there of.

After the dust settled I realized, shattered ego and all, that even though he and I were not "together" in a romantic relationship, we had managed to forge a friendship. We had a relationship of honesty—even when it hurt, loyalty, companionship, and best of all laughter. We laughed at our many mistakes and triumphant failures.

We provided much needed, though at times unwanted, *Dear Abby* type of advice to each other, me more so than him because he was indeed a ladies' man. I quickly learned that the bag of tricks I employed was not too different from a lot of my girlfriends', or even the women he was dating, bag of tricks.

Although our relationship did not lead to marriage, I learned a lot. I'm thankful that we did not get married, it would have been a mistake. Still, it pains me to think that he, or other well intending "good" men (my brother included) will end up with women that add nothing of value their lives but an orgasm. So, I decided to package all the late night calls, text messages, and emails about dating advice that we both shared in a simple concept that I call *Pockets & Panties*. The intent is to provide insight and guidance from a female perspective. The hope is that the words, stories and caveats will help you choose the right woman.

XO
Canise

THE CONCEPT

POCKETS & PANTIES reveals the underlying intentions of women in romantic heterosexual relationships. In talking to girlfriends, guy-friends, and observing friends of friends I realized that a male's primary goal as it relates to women in dating relationships is to obtain self-esteem (ego) and sexual gratification via intercourse and the female's primary goal is to obtain security via financial stability.

In any romantic relationship -serious or whimsical- both parties are interlocked in a game that converges at different points in their strategic plans. In order to reach their ultimate goals women devise and execute stealthy plans that involve getting into a man's **head**, then his **heart,** and finally his ***Pockets***. On the contrary, men go through a woman's **head**, then **heart**, to get to her ***Panties***.

Many believe that men are from Mars and women are from Venus. While I am not challenging the planetary origins of each, I do believe that men and women speak different languages. *Pockets & Panties* is the intersection of both worlds and cast light on the underlying motivations of men and women. *Pockets & Panties* breaks the language barrier and sets the record straight about how a woman manipulates her way through the dating game to reach her goals.

Pockets & Panties

For men it is all about the panties. Romance, companionship and other things are often times just the collateral damage of a man's pursuit of the *Panties*. Women, on the other hand, will give up the panties in order to obtain their ultimate prize…*Pockets*. Neither however is usually honest enough with herself, himself or the other party to reveal this in the beginning of the dating game. Thus, each manipulates the other and plays an infamous game of cat and mouse to get either the *Pockets* or *Panties*.

WHY YOU NEED THIS BOOK

To help you become a proficient game player and to avoid the high stakes of relationships (hurt emotions, finances, health etc.) each chapter in *Pockets & Panties* addresses specific rules of the game. Commit each of them to memory and refer to them often. Like the game Monopoly, once you fully understand the rules/caveats, you will have a better chance of navigating the treacherous mines of the dating field with minimal casualties, collecting your $200, passing go, and winning "the game."

Have you ever dated someone that disrespected you, used you for your money, broke your heart or otherwise did you wrong? Ever wondered why each new woman reminds you of your ex? It is simply because many times people repeat the same vicious cycle when it comes to dating. This cycle in-turn produces dating prospects with similar qualities that your ex may have had. Birds of a feather can usually be found at similar ponds.

A clear understanding of the opposite sex is a prerequisite to fully understand the game. *Pockets & Panties* offers a detailed analysis of the male/female romantic relationship, and is framed for males from a female perspective. This analysis enables even the shy or inexperienced to navigate and play the game like a professional. *Pockets & Panties* uncovers and identifies the traps so that they can be avoided.

II. THE FINE PRINT

Caveat Emptor (**kav**-ee-aht **emp**-taw) is a Latin phrase that means, "Let the buyer beware." When purchasing a large ticket item, it only makes sense to take heed to the return policy. The onus is on the consumer to test quality, warranty, and return policies before purchasing something of value. A wise consumer will ensure that the product has all of the desired features before making a purchasing decision. A wise consumer will also be sure to read the fine print as often times when a product looks too good to be true it usually is. Dating is no different.

Similar to reading the fine print before making a purchase that could lead to regret, it is equally important to know the caveats of the dating game. Game? Yes! Everyone knows that dating is a game but not everyone knows how to play the game. In the game Monopoly, the person with the most houses, hotels, and money wins. An unsuspecting novice player may find himself bankrupt and in jail if he does not pay attention to what the other players are doing or buying. The same is true for male and female romantic relationships. The games that men and women play consist of several rules and caveats that are essential to know, understand and actively practice. It would behoove you to know the game and play it well otherwise, you will get played.

DEFINITIONS

There are a few words that are commonly used liberally in that the meaning changes depending on several factors. To clarify how some liberally used words are used in *Pockets & Panties* they are defined below:

Relationship
A connectedness between two people. The parameters of will determine what type of relationship exists.

Friend
Like the word nice, "friend" is one of the most overused words in the English language. Everybody is a "friend," exaggeratingly speaking. Even when you meet someone new, almost immediately s/he is introduced as a "friend." People even use "friend" to describe someone they have had sex with when there was never a committed relationship with the person. Also, knowing someone for a significant amount of time can lead to deeming a person as a "friend" simply because s/he has been around for so long. There are countless definitions for the word friend. Still, people use it haphazardly. A friendship requires mutual trust, respect, and loyalty. I do not believe that most men and women can "just" be friends. The operative word here is "just." Of course men and women will have relationships (as defined above). However, a significant number of those relationships will involve sex (as defined below) or have sexual undertones. Because men and women have different motivations it is quite difficult for the two to ever genuinely connect on a purely platonic level; sex or sexual attraction will always get in the way.

The examples in *Pockets & Panties* are real. To protect the innocent…and the guilty "friend" is used in lieu of names when illustrating examples of those that shall remain anonymous. Thus a "friend" is a person I know, have known, heard of or read about, or even myself.

Sex
An act that involves one or both parties being aroused and sexually satisfied by the other. Vaginal penetration is not a prerequisite for a sexual relationship. Oral sex, fondling or heavy petting is included.

Rebound
A relationship that occurs shortly after a break-up. Rebound relationships can begin before an official break-up; especially if one partner has begun to distance him/herself emotionally. Rebound relationships rarely go the distance as they are typically used as a distraction or coping mechanism from the emotional pain of a break-up.

Sexting
The act of sending sexually explicit text messages, pictures, or videos usually via mobile phones.

Emotional Blackmail
A very powerful form of manipulation wherein someone close to you threatens to punish you if you do not give in to his/her demands.

There are also several references to movies, which for many women, are like bibles. If you have not previously seen *Bridget Jones Diary*, *Love Jones* or *When Harry Met Sally*, I submit that watching them could certainly improve your understanding of women as well.

Canise Gray

Rule 1: What You See Is What You Get

Sometimes, appearances can be deceiving. However, in some ways---when it comes to women, what you see is really what you get. You just have to know what to look for.

A WOMAN'S CLOTHING says a lot about her. Paying close attention to a woman's wardrobe will reveal just about anything you ever wanted, or did not want to know, about her. Every single detail of a woman's ensemble says something about her. Everything!

Some say that women get dressed for other women. In some cases that may be true. However, in most cases, women get dressed for men. From the high heel shoes that hurt our feet, the spanks that tighten our mid-sections, to the push-up bras that make our cleavage look ever so inviting, all of these uncomfortable and revealing things women wear is to gain the attention of men.

Women do not spend countless hours getting our hair colored, relaxed, weaved, braided or twisted and our eyebrows, legs, and other womanly parts waxed, plucked, threaded, or laser-ed so that another woman can compliment us. Women do not have liposuction, butt implants, or wear panty pads to give our butts a round shape so other women will approach us. Women do all of these time consuming, expensive and sometimes even painful things because we believe that these are the things that *men* want. Women do these things because we think, and rightfully so, that if we look a certain way we will have a better chance of getting what we really want--a man, but more specifically into a man's Pockets.

Rather consciously or subconsciously, whatever it is that you seek, you will ultimately find. This concept is the very reason why men approach certain women and ignore or, are indifferent towards others. In your journey toward a compatible relationship, you should find that the type of women you are drawn to are remarkably different toward the latter end of the journey than the women that caught your attention early on. No one really wants to be the old man in a club. And, personally I am convinced that no one truly wants to die alone. As men mature and become "ready to settle down" I have observed that they begin to value more in a woman than what she does in the sheets.

Thus, when you are looking to spend your life with someone, physical attraction, although a factor, cannot be the most important factor. If you are seeking women to add as preverbal notches to a belt, you will be drawn to the woman who looks, or at least dresses like notch number **X**, Why? When a lion hunts prey, they often go after sickly, young, or old victims…EASY prey. Like the king of the jungle, men employ the same hunting techniques with women. With several successful "hunts" men mentally associate provocative looks with sexual outcomes, hence, what they see, is what they get!

Now, imagine getting a call from your friend just as you are preparing to leave work. He invites you to a happy hour. You think about offering some lame excuse for not going because you are really drained. The more you think about it your decision sways toward attending. Your decision to attend is not based on the number of drink or appetizer specials. Your decision to attend is based on either your desire not to say no to your friend, or your desire to meet women. Whatever your reason for deciding to tag along, women will surely be there to meet you.

Now imagine that you go to an after work happy hour and see a woman in a low v-cut, cleavage spilling, form fitting blue dress. Let's call her "Devil in the Blue Dress" *(DBD)*. By design you naturally think of her physique and what you could possibly do with or to it. Instead play the game, think twice, and proceed with caution! If you are playing the game you should be thinking:

- Did she wear that to work?
- What type of job does she have where such an ensemble is permissible?
- Does she even have a job?
- If she does have a job, did she go home and change clothes in order to a wear such a revealing dress to an after work happy hour?

Not asking yourself these types of questions leaves you susceptible to the games the DBD certainly will play with you as discussed later in the book. Keep reading!

Sure the DBD is attractive, stunning even. She has all the right curves in all the right places. Her hair is just the way you like it. All of your friends would admire you if you had her on your arm because, after all, she is gorgeous. Let's think about this though, a woman in a tight and revealing dress at an after work happy hour or professional networking event is there for one thing. No that one thing is not to "hook-up" with a guy like you. She is there for Pockets! Whether yours or some other unsuspecting gentleman who also finds her dress and curves impressive. She thoroughly knows the ins and outs of the game, thus she will likely get exactly what she came for.

The rapper T.I. penned a popular song some years ago with the catchy hook "You can have whatever you like." The song had become somewhat of a female fantasy anthem. Why?

Because women like things…flashy, sparkly, designer-labeled things. More importantly some women like those things more when they do not have to pay for them with their own money.

The type of shoes, purses, clothes, and jewelry a woman wears reveals a lot about who she is. Everybody loves designer labels but not everybody can afford designer labels. When you meet a woman that is outfitted almost exclusively in designer labels, it is best to evaluate how she got them. Does she have the salary to afford the Gucci handbag, the Tiffany Necklace, the Christian Louboutin shoes? Is she a **Poser**, a ***Professional Dater*** or a **Go Getter**?

Poser—A Poser is the type of woman that brags about the designer things she has. If she does have designer purses she will usually have the signature series (the design with the logos all over the bag) so that everyone will know the brand of bag that she is carrying. A Poser loves designer names and will use them as proper nouns frequently in lieu of general item descriptions.

For instance, a Poser will say "Gucci Purse" instead of just saying purse. You know this person is a Poser because she is not accustomed to having designer items and thus feels the need to remind everyone else-- by using proper nouns--that she has a designer item. A Poser may have some designer items but there is little consistency when viewing her wardrobe in totality.

A woman that has to have a designer bag but does not have matching undergarments or bed linens, or has designer shoes and swap meet earrings is a Poser. If she is living from check to check trying to keep up an image, then she is a Poser. The Poser is more concerned with what others think about how she looks than how she is as a person. A Poser is typically extremely superficial. Therefore, the Poser may even save money in order to purchase one key designer item, or a few designer items that she feels will propel her to an elevated social status. Her motto is, "Pass my Gucci Purse."

Professional Dater: A Professional Dater is a woman that "dates" men in order for them to finance her lifestyle. By "date" I mean have a sexual relationship. She may swear that she is not sexually involved with the men that pay her rent or purchase large ticket gift items. However, if you were to dig enough, you would surely find dirt. A Professional Dater uses sex, or the promise of sex, in exchange for favors.

The Professional Dater is the type of woman that has to have a man. She will go on dates just to get a free meal.
You know you are dealing with a Professional Dater when she has countless designer items that she has not paid for.
The red flag for you is when she talks about what her other boyfriends did for her. Whether trips, lavish gifts, or paying her bills; she will tell you about her ex boyfriends in terms of what they did for her and what she expects you to do for her.

The Professional Dater may have designer digs but like the Poser, her designer taste is inconsistent. What she actually purchases herself will often be less expensive than what she has swindled from men that she has been sexually involved with. The Professional Dater is also materialistic but when it comes to her own money she is much more frugal. Her motto is, "Everything is better when someone else is paying for it."

Go-Getter: A Go-Getter is a woman with discriminating taste. She knows what she wants and works hard and smart to get it. She is the type of woman that may have a few designer items; in some cases she may even have a lot of designer items. The thing that distinguishes her from the Posers and Professional Daters is that the Go-Getter is consistent.

This particular type of woman may have had to cut corners to build her credit score and maintain some money in the bank. She is the type of woman that will make sure her bills are paid and pay herself by saving before going out to purchase designer items. A Go-Getter's appearance and style of dress can range from K-Mart to Kate Spade.

What differentiates a Go-Getter from her female counterparts is not the label inside her shoes. Rather, it is the consistency in all her spending habits. For example, a Go-Getter will pay her mortgage before paying for a Louis Vuitton purse. It is not that a Go-Getter will not have designer label taste or even have designer-labeled items. If she does however, her credit score, bank accounts, and other monthly fiscal responsibilities will not be in default because of it. You will know that you are dealing with a Go-Getter if she is unwilling to exchange sexual favors or compromise herself for monetary payments or gifts. Her motto is, "I work hard for the money, so you better treat me right!"

RESIDENCE

You can also learn a lot about a woman by where she resides. When evaluating her place of residence, you must take into account the totality of circumstances. So, merely knowing her address or zip code will not reveal as much as you think. If you make conclusions based on an address or zip code alone, you may discredit someone that could be a potential match for you.

Consider the following scenarios to determine which type of woman (Poser, Professional Dater, or Go-Getter) lives at each residence.

Residence One is a hip new luxury condo. The building is within walking distance of public transportation, shops and restaurants. The amenities include a 24-hour concierge service, controlled access, indoor pool, fitness center, and garage parking.

Residence Two is an end unit townhome in a 200-unit community that combines the best of classic architecture with modern amenities. The community has been certified by the U.S. Green Building Council as being more environmentally friendly and energy efficient than typical new homes.

Residence Three is a single family dwelling in one of the city's transitioning neighborhoods. The security features include iron bars on all of the windows, and iron gates on the front and back doors. The economic disparities are seen through the hodgepodge of older model cars parked on the street. The retail companies in the area are limited to a 24-hour laundry and a mom and pop convenience store.

Based on the above information alone one might probably conclude that the Poser lives in *Residence Three*, the Professional Dater lives in *Residence Two*, and the Go Getter lives in *Residence One*. However, arriving at such a conclusion would be dead wrong.

The Poser could very well be living check-to-check and destroying her credit rating by living in *Residence One* to keep up appearances. *Residence Two* could be a mixed-use development funded by the Department of Housing and

Urban Development that offers some HCVP (a.k.a. Section 8) rental units—and the home of a Professional Dater. The Go-Getter could in fact live *Residence Three*. The home may be completely renovated and be within the latest gentrification zone in the city. Remember, a residence includes more than a physical address or a zip code. *What you see is what you get* but the more you see the more you will know.

Thus with residence, its not so much where a woman lives, but rather how she lives. Does her monthly living expenses exceed her net income? Was her furniture purchased on credit or by other men she has dated? These are the types of questions that you will want to uncover the answers to in order to fully understand the type of woman she is.

RESTAURANTS

A friend told me a story about a woman he once met. The woman was very attractive and he was drawn to her. He told her that he would give her anything she wanted. One day he asked her where she would like to eat. He told her that he would take her anywhere she wanted to go.

Her response was, "Anywhere?"
"Sure baby," he said.
She replied, "Ooooh I wanna go to Fridays!"

True story! Needless to say the relationship was short-lived. My friend was looking for a Go-Getter and she certainly was not the one.

Paying attention to the dining choices a woman is inclined to make can tell you something about the type of woman she is. The woman my friend described above had never been or had rarely been to Friday's.

You can infer a few different things about a grown woman that has never been to Friday's including, but by no means limited to:
   1. She has a sophisticated palette and does not frequent a chain restaurant and prefers local and organic cuisine;
   2. She prefers to cook her meals either because of food dietary allergies or taste; or
   3. That her idea of going out to eat involves a drive-thru window.

My friend of course inferred number three. Friday's is not the type of dining establishment that will easily impress a Go-Getter. A Go-Getter may go to Friday's with her girlfriends. She may even order take out from Friday's but she will not, however, be impressed by a man taking her to Friday's on a date. She would not aspire to dine at Friday's because such dining would already be within her reach. Thus when asked to pick any restaurant in the city for dinner, Friday's would not be a likely response.

Does all this mean that you should be impressed with a woman that wants you to take her only to five-star dining establishments? Does it mean that you should not date a woman that is impressed by Fridays? It really depends on you and what you are looking for. Given the question my friend posed, he expected the woman to reach beyond her own grasp so-to-speak. He wanted to know what restaurant the woman wanted to visit that maybe finances or circumstances had not allowed. Thus, Friday's was the wrong answer for the kind of woman he was looking for.

SOCIAL INTERACTIONS

Lastly, how a woman behaves socially, whether in real life or on social media applications, can tell you an awful lot about her. In statistics, an outlier is an observation that is numerically distant from the rest of the data. In dating, an outlier is a behavior that is distinctly different from the desired perception. The outlier perception always becomes the reality. An example of outlier behavior is a woman that is extremely nice to you but has poor etiquette or is rude to others.

If you take a woman to dinner and she goes off on the server or is otherwise rude, snide or the like, do not dismiss the behavior or excuse it. She is showing you who she really is. If you give a woman a gift and she is unappreciative - does not say thank you, asks for something else or asks you where is the rest- do not discount the behavior or make excuses.

Any woman that has not learned proper social graces only spells trouble down the line. As it relates to social media, be cautious of women that post their entire lives for "friends" and "followers" to see. I also suggest you steer clear of women with racy or otherwise sexually explicit pictures posted. While I do not profess to be a psychologist, counselor, or preacher, I submit that the need for constant validation, likes, etc. from "friends" and "followers" may be a symptom of a much larger problem. *What you see is what you get*...for better or worse.

Rule 2: Women Are Just Like Men

Forget everything you know, or think you know about women and dating, seriously. Women have a phenomenal marketing campaign. Since the beginning of time, we have somehow managed to convince men that we are dainty, helpless, good, loyal and any other adjective you can conjure up to go along with the sugar and spice and everything nice ideology. If you think back to the very first woman, Eve, even she was cunning. Every woman, whether she admits it or not, has a deceptive twin within. What matters the most is how she uses her.

When you first meet a woman, she is going to put her best Jimmy Choo foot forward. The same way that you go out of your way to show her what you think she wants, she does the same to you. She will go out of her way to present a flawless appearance, charming personality and even a level of loyalty. This is the getting-to-know-you stage of the relationship. Good behavior is critical in this stage because without it, she is unable to get what she wants, you and ultimately your Pockets.

The Rotation

You will rarely meet a woman that is not involved with another man. Rather romantic or whimsical, women have rotations. She may tell you that she has friends, but Rob Schneider's 1989 blockbuster hit, *When Harry Met Sally,* portrays it the best ---- men and women simply cannot be friends. Adults cannot *just* be friends because sexual attraction always gets in the way. There are typically only four types of male friends that a woman has.

A Gay Friend is seemingly self-explanatory but I'll explain anyway. The Gay Friend is the guy that is there to listen to all the relationship drama and give advice. Women learn a lot from gay men. Everything from sex to style is up for discussion.

A Fantasy Friend is the friend that is not a friend at all. The fantasy friend is the guy that women refer to as friends because they are too embarrassed to admit that the relationship is purely sexual in nature. The fantasy friend is the guy that women have sex with (oral, anal, or vaginal) without having a commitment. He is the guy that sends late night texts messages and makes frequent late night pit stops for sexual gratification. Depending on the duration of the relationship, she may also refer to him as an ex–boyfriend or even a fiancé. The Fantasy Friend is no more than a glorified booty call, random, or jump-off.

A Forever Friend is a little more complicated. In the Forever Friend relationship, both parties care about each other deeply. The dynamics of the relationship will vary depending on the specific circumstances. The one control factor in the Forever Friend relationship is that the two are not currently in a mutually exclusive romantic relationship. Sex is not always involved in a Forever Friendship but, , the two may have been sexually involved. What is certain in a Forever Friendship is that during some point in the relationship; either one or both parties thought about and maybe even pursued romantic or sexual involvement. Even when both parties are romantically involved with someone else, a Forever Friend can suck the life out of a potentially viable romantic relationship. A Forever Friend could be a legitimate ex boyfriend or husband. Wonder who the Forever Friend is? Reviewing the call log in a woman's cell phone will quickly reveal the culprit. I am not advocating you check a woman's phone records, without her permission of course. That would simply be uncouth. However, unless boundaries and limitations are clearly defined, a Forever Friend most certainly spells trouble.

A Friend in Waiting is a friendship that is patiently waiting for the right time to become more. Either the man or woman wants more but the timing simply is not right. Friends in Waiting may communicate as much as Forever Friends. The Friends in Waiting are all of the men in a woman's contact list. She keeps them around because she likes them or they may like her. Either way one of the two is waiting for the just the right time to make a move.

Have you ever ended a relationship and heard just a few days or weeks later that your ex was with someone new? If so, she didn't suddenly meet someone fabulous. The new guy was around the majority of the time if not the entire time. He may be a Friend in Waiting that she called to catch up with. He could also be a Fantasy Friend that sent a late night text message at just the right time.

Have you ever been in a long distance relationship and noticed that your significant other spent a lot of time with a male friend? When women spend a significant amount of time with another man alone i.e. not in a group setting, he is most likely a Fantasy or Forever Friend.

Adults do not typically or easily make new friends of the opposite sex. Of course, there are some exceptions but when it comes to men and women, a *friend* must fall into one of the above categories. Whenever a woman describes another man as her *friend*, your antennas should go up. If you are dating someone that you are serious about be sure to pay close attention to the *friend* interaction in order to determine which type of *friend* the guy is. Women keep these friends in rotation for various reasons.

THE LYING GAME

When it comes to telling lies, women are not just like men, we are even better! We spend most of our lives perfecting the craft. Think about it. Seriously!

Have you ever seen a woman cry to get what she wants? Sure you have. She learned at an early age that if she cried she could get her way. In relationships, when all else fails, an immature woman will pull the emotional card and cry a river in order to get her way.

Women lie in the beginning, middle, and end of relationships, for different reasons. In the beginning, women lie to make themselves look good. Sometimes even how she looks is a lie. From the lace front wig or hair weave, spanks, fake eyelashes, fingernails, concealer and make-up, to her push-up bra, padded panties, or even butt lift, the appearance can be less than authentic to yield what women may think is a desired look.

Women will also lie in the beginning of a relationship to impress and attract men. When you first meet a woman you really are meeting her representative…her spokesperson. It takes several months, years even, to get to really know someone—especially when people make elaborate efforts to suppress who they really are.

In the getting-to-know-you-stage, women lie because they want to appear nonchalant. Take something as simple as calling her. If you do not call her when you said you would in the beginning of a courtship, she says things like "it is ok" or "no big-deal." She lies!

It is a big deal, it is always a big deal. You know it is a big deal because when you are in fact in a relationship a woman will fuss and complain about it. In the getting-to-know-you-stage however she just does not want to appear to be that interested or concerned. So….she will lie.

Women love to give the impression that they have so many other things on their minds, so they pretend to be unfazed when you do not call. However women *do* get upset when the phone does not ring/vibrate. Towards the middle and end of the relationship true feelings will surface about how a woman feels. "It is ok" and "no big deal" will become, "Why didn't you call?" or worse they will place men on Panty Punishment. Panty Punishment is when a woman withholds sex simply because she did not get her way.

Think about it. In the beginning, women will try to portray somewhat of a modest image. Many women do not want men to know—at least in the beginning—that they are promiscuous. The woman that you are interested in may not want you to know that she had sex in the back of a car, or in a restaurant bathroom with a previous partner on date one. Why? It's simple, you are the new guy. She still has a chance to get you to treat her differently. A friend recently shared a post about a woman that had been a professional prostitute. She changed her life and became very religious. In doing so she found a husband. Unfortunately for him, she did not reveal that prior to her transformation she was paid for sex…for a living. Of course, not every woman is promiscuous but the women that are; will most likely lie about it…at least in the beginning. Don't blame her. Promiscuous women are not given the same respect as their male counterparts.

Pockets & Panties

In the middle of a relationship, women will lie to spare men's feelings. Women will lie about how many men they have had sex with and about past relationships. They also lie about these things to portray a more conservative image of themselves. Women love telling men that this guy or that guy is just a friend. What they fail to tell men is that the guy was a Fantasy Friend (defined above). No matter how innocent or demure you think a woman is, she is always going to have someone on the back burner. Yes, A-L-W-A-Y-S.

I know plenty women that professed that they have never had sex. These women are well into their twenties and thirties. It is the Clinton-esque type of lie. These women have had oral and anal sex! But they profess that they have never had sex. They rationalize that they are telling the truth. Anyone with half a brain knows that oral and anal sex constitute sex. Just because they claim (I do not believe that part either) to have never been penetrated vaginally, they profess to have never had sex before.

When it comes to sex, the classic lie women tell is "I've never done that before." Sometimes you may actually come across someone that is inexperienced sexually. However, if a woman tells you that she has never done *that* before, yet she is comfortable doing *that* with you and she just met you, she is probably lying.

To protect your feelings she will also lie about how great sex is with you. Read any women's magazine and you will discover countless articles about women faking orgasms. Surveys such as the National Orgasm Survey (I am not making this up—this is a real survey http://tiny.cc/cgpap1) revealed that almost 50% of women claim to never achieve a vaginal orgasm. Yet ask any man and he will swear that a woman has never faked an orgasm with him. Because most women tell these lies and are better at faking an orgasm than Meg Ryan in *When Harry Met Sally*, every man goes around thinking he is great in bed, but when considering the number of women who fake it, it is simply mathematically impossible.

Remember, she is just like you and she will also lie to protect her own hide. If you have ever been in a relationship and been cheated on, you probably didn't even know it. You really would not know unless you were looking for it. What you seek, you usually find; but unlike men, women are detail oriented and do a much better job at concealing indiscretions.

Women can have a rotation that includes a boyfriend, Fantasy Friends, Forever Friends and Friends in Waiting. A woman's friendship trifecta is usually aware that the boyfriend exists. By definition each knows his role and may even know the boyfriend personally. Thus, the woman typically only has to lie to one person…the boyfriend. So, it is a lot easier for her to keep up with her lies. Because she does not have to lie to the other guys, she can take a call from the boyfriend with her friend in arm's reach.

A woman that I know was in a long-distance relationship for several years. Her boyfriend thought things were going well. He always sent gifts, called consistently and spoke highly of her. When her boyfriend called she would only talk a few minutes before she had to end the call. However, she always managed to make time for her Friend in Waiting. Not before long, the Friend in Waiting became her new boyfriend. The unknowingly ex-boyfriend found out when he made a surprise visit to the girlfriend and found her walking up to her apartment with her new boyfriend toting a bottle of wine.

To the ex-boyfriend things happened seemingly suddenly. In relationships though things are never that simple. His girlfriend didn't wake up that morning and decide she no longer wanted to be with him. In fact, even after that incident she kept him in her contact list, as a Forever/Fantasy Friend of course. Over the course of the relationship she lied to him habitually to keep her rotation going. All of the unanswered calls, text messages, etc. were not just happenstance. Her brief conversations and incessant unavailability were definite hints that she was not ready for an exclusive relationship with him. He simply missed all the signs.

OPPORTUNITY KNOCKS

The system was designed for women to be opportunistic. Nowadays, there are TV shows that highlight how successful some women have become by having sex with a famous man or marrying and divorcing a famous man. From The *Real Housewives* series –a show that profiles many women that have achieved fame, status, or financial gain from the men they have had sex with--to the ever so popular *Love & Hip Hop* series that features more girlfriends and baby mommas than wives, and more recently even *Hollywood Exes*, there are tons of examples of *Pockets & Panties* at work in real life.

Canise Gray

I know several friends that only date men of a certain height and size so that they have a better chance of birthing the next athletic superstar. How many times have you seen a beautiful woman with a very unattractive man and wondered, "How did he get her"? Well, he most likely got her attention because he was willing to shower her with gifts, pay her bills, or finance her lifestyle in some other way. Even a financially secure woman can be charmed by an unattractive, equally or more financially secure man. A woman will stay with an unattractive man when, (1) he treats her like she wants to be treated, or (2) yields the money or power to giver her the life she wants.
In other words, the bigger the *Pockets* the lower the aesthetic standards can be.

Chris Rock once stated, "Every time a man is being nice to you, all he's doing is offering [sex]." The opposite is not true. Women are naturally nice or cordial but if a woman goes out of her way for a man it is not out of the kindness of her heart. Whenever a woman does something to place a man's interest before her own, there is usually something in it for her. There may not be immediate gratification because women are willing to wait for a reward. Women will go the extra mile if they believe that they will benefit in the long run.

RULE 3: ALL WOMEN WANT MONEY

Tune in to a few cable television networks, on any night of the week, and you are bound to find a show dedicated to brides. As a matter of fact WE network at one time highlighted "Wedding Sunday's" and advertised it as, "The destination for the best unscripted wedding shows on television!"

From *Bridezillas*, *Four Weddings*, *Platinum Weddings*, *My Fair Wedding*, and *Say Yes to the Dress*, there are multiple programs that show women as monsters willing to do anything to have a celebrity style wedding. Blame it on the editing if you choose, but it is no coincidence that the women are depicted spending money they do not have in order to have an elaborate fairytale wedding.

The wedding industry is a billion dollar industry. Many women dream of their wedding day. Some have the entire affair planned from the dress to the flower arrangements well before encountering the fiancé. Women dream about the day they will transition from the prefix "Ms." to "Mrs." They anxiously wait for the day that they can permanently replace the title of friend, boyfriend and fiancé with husband.

This idea that a man/husband will miraculously erase a woman's problems and provide a fairytale life can be traced all the way back to a childhood story. . . Cinderella.

Storyline: The story begins with a girl performing manual labor all the while desiring a better life. A Prince invites all of the young ladies in town to a ball so that he may choose a bride. The entire town swarms the ball, and Cinderella is crying in despair because she does not have the proper attire to attend the ball. She is supernaturally transformed into a stately beauty by her fairy godmother. Her clothes are magically transformed into a beautiful evening gown and she is outfitted with a coach to usher her to the ball. Cinderella's magical adornments are only temporary. The Prince meets Cinderella, he becomes entranced; and you know the rest! Cinderella marries the Prince and gets the life that she so desperately wanted.

This well-known classic folk tale of Cinderella can be traced back to as early as 6 B.C. So, even before the adoption of the Gregorian calendar; women have been indoctrinated to believe that somehow, even magically, we will be swept off of our feet and taken care of by a Prince. In the classic fairy tale, Cinderella and the Prince had only known each other for 48 hours when he concluded that he just had to have her. He wanted her because she was pretty. It didn't matter that she only had rags for clothing or a pumpkin as a coach. She was pretty and that was enough for the Prince.

Cinderella didn't know much about the Prince either. However, she knew that she had to put up a facade in order to get his attention. She knew that a Prince would not give her a second look if he met her in the rags that she wore. Cinderella was a phony and everything about her was fake! She knew that she couldn't get the prince by being herself; so she portrayed an image that would draw his attention. Her story is not about love. It is about the inner most motivations of women in romantic relationships.

Cinderella wasn't interested in the Prince because she loved him. Cinderella really wanted the life that she knew the Prince could provide. Cinderella knew that if the Prince was in her life, she would never have to scrub another floor or wear another rag. Marrying the Prince meant that she would have a coach, horsemen, glass slippers and evening gowns that didn't expire at midnight. The story unfortunately ends with Cinderella and the Prince living happily ever after and women have based ideas about romantic relationships on a flawed concept that a woman's job is to look pretty and a man's job is to take care of her. Maybe we can blame it on Cinderella that women want men to provide them with financial security and a fairy tale ending.

Whatever it is that women say they want in a man usually comes down to money. The security desired really boils down to knowing that she has a roof over her head, jewelry, cars, vacations, shopping sprees, bills paid etc. All of those *things* require substantial financial outputs. Even though women deny it [or do not realize it], the desire for a man usually comes down to financial security and, like Cinderella, women will go to great lengths to transform themselves in order to get a fairytale ending.

A close girlfriend called me to complain about one of her friends being a Professional Dater. She explained that the friend had been on trips, had men paying her bills, and had a closet filled with new clothes all on some man's dime. My friend was upset because she had just spent $75.00 on a pair of shoes after waiting several months for them to go on sale. While she was driving back from the mall her girlfriend called her to brag about what one of her Fantasy Friends purchased for her. My friend was livid, as she complained about all of the things that she had to purchase on her own. She was not willing to compromise her morality in order to get a man to spend his money on her. Even though my friend is highly educated and gainfully employed, she still longed for a man to do all the things for her that she is very capable of doing herself. Why? Because all women--whether they admit it or not-- want financial security.

Because women generally have antiquated fairy tale ideas about romantic relationships, consciously or subconsciously they focus on money (*Pockets*). Remember our devil in the blue dress from *Rule One*? A man that approaches her is most likely going to offer to buy her a drink (*Pockets*). After a few drinks and a conversation; they may make plans for an evening out on the town, where he will certainly be expected to pick up the tab (even more *Pockets!*).

There is not much that can be done to change how women view the male role in a romantic relationship. The best scenario is to find a woman that is willing to share what's in her purse and not always dig into your Pockets. Keep reading and I'll tell you how to get there.

III. THE PARADIGM

Before moving forward let's quickly recap the Rules.

1. What You See is What You Get -- Women go through elaborate measures to present a flawless image to potential suitors. No matter how elaborate the measure though, if you look close enough you will surely know what you are getting yourself into before you go too deep. Pay attention to the subtleties and look for consistency.

2. Women Are Just Like Men -- Women will lie, cheat, and steal to get what they want --a man to take care of them. All is fair in love and war! Believe only half of what you see and nothing she says until her actions demonstrate that she is trustworthy.

3. All Women Want Money -- Sure women want romance and security but both of those things cost money. She may be content with what she has now but she will always want more. After all she is a fe[e]-male. Whoever said the best things in life are free obviously never had a clue. Everything cost money and women are no different. Be careful to find a woman who wants you as well as your money. You need a woman who will share what's in her purse with what's in your Pockets.

Now that you are equipped with the 3 caveats, we are ready to delve into the fundamental concepts of Pockets & Panties Head →Heart →Pockets.

It is not checkers, it is chess! Women are not going to walk up to you and say, "This is a stick up!" Do you think that they're going to tell you how much they cost upfront? Unless you are dealing with an escort, things will be much more subtle than that. It is a process for women to gain the ultimate goal. However, the first step in the process is to get into a man's head. It is usually done by the subtle things that they say, what they wear etc. It is not beyond women to use scare tactics to get into a man's head either. Women will utilize pregnancy scares to sudden job offers that require them to move miles away in order to gain some aspect of control over your thought process. Women are Just Like Men (Caveat 2) but they are more organized when it comes to lying.

Head Games: Don't Believe Everything You Think

Head Game #1 Crying

WHEN ALL ELSE FAILS, some women cry in order to get what they want. They are fully aware that the average man hates to see a woman cry, and they will use this tactic to gain the attention, time or favor of a potential suitor. The point is to display some level of vulnerability in order for the man to do the same. Whether the crying is from real or imagined drama, it is to eviscerate a certain response from the man.

I know a woman that has a crying routine specifically for the first time that she has sex with a new guy. Yes...really! How does it work? When she meets a guy, they do the usual song and dance-- sending each other text messages for the first few days. The text messages are usually flirty in nature. Eventually, the guy asks her to come over or to "hang out" but she plays the unavailable game (See Head Game #3). When the guy asks her on a legitimate date, she usually agrees to a date. After dinner and a few drinks both are relaxed and begin to let guards down.

On the drive back to her house, of course he asks the proverbial question, "Mind if I come in?" She bashfully agrees. All the while, he's thinking that he's a lucky man because she agreed to let him in. Little does he know that letting him in was part of her plan from the beginning.

Once he's in, the fondling becomes more intense and the two eventually have sex. Exhausted, he falls asleep in her bed. When he's preparing to leave during the middle of the night, she acts as if she is mortified. She asks him if they had sex, as if she is unaware. When he replies "Yes!" she acts as if she is in disbelief. She becomes hysterical and explains how she has never slept with a guy so soon. Crying and distraught, she sits in her bed, naked, hoping that he will comfort her--hoping he will fall for her antics. When he puts his clothes down and walks back to the bed, she knows that she has him…hook, line, and sinker!

Several of my friends admitted to lying about someone dying in order to get a man's attention. Yes! These women actually told men that someone close to them died, just so the men would stay on the phone longer, or better yet...come over. Some of the women rationalized that they were not lying if they didn't say when the person died. For instance, one friend told a guy that her grandmother died. Sure her grandmother had died-- several years earlier. The imagined drama got her exactly what she wanted though-- sympathy and more quality time.

One of my friends had a woman in his rotation that he kept around frankly because she had a big butt—butts are *in* these days. He reached a point in his life where he realized that he had to do some pruning in order to really grow. This woman was not sophisticated enough for him. In fact, she was very simple. He eventually decided that he had to let this particular woman go.

Prior to his decision, the relationship consisted of sexually explicit text and chat messages and sporadic dinners. When he stopped responding to her text and chat messages, her messages became even more frequent and intense. This particular woman started sending messages incessantly. Initially, the messages read of concern because she had not heard from my friend in a while. When my friend didn't respond, the woman started down her emotional tirade. She sent profane messages indicating that she couldn't believe that he dumped her (See Chapter 5, Women Create Their Own Relationships). Then, the woman started sending very detailed messages explaining how she had been sexually molested and never once thought that she would have a chance to fall in love like she did with my friend. She went on and on about all her emotional baggage and pleaded that my friend call her back because she couldn't stop crying over him. She even went as far as asking him to marry her... over a text message! Luckily, my friend knew the Head→Heart→Pockets theory and didn't fall for her Head Games.

It is important to note that this particular woman had serious emotional issues. The messages that she sent were red flags showing that she was extremely emotionally unstable. Had he given in, just to get to the *Panties*, there's no telling what tricks she would have employed to trap him.

Head Game #2 Secrets

HOW MANY WOMEN DO YOU KNOW that can keep a secret? Even in our female friendships, women divulge confidential and embarrassing things about girlfriends even when they promise to keep lips sealed. Every guy that has ever had a serious relationship with a woman knows more than he would care to know about his girlfriend's family members and friends. Why? For women, keeping a secret is telling it to someone that they think will not tell it to someone else. However, a secret can be kept between three people, only when two are dead.

Whenever a woman claims to be telling you a secret—something she has never told anyone else before, especially in the getting-to-know-you phase, be cautious. Think about it? How often do people reveal innermost secrets to someone they barely know?

Try to have sex with women to soon and the first thing they say is "I do not know you yet" or "I do not know you like that." The same woman that proclaims how much she does not know a man will tell the same man an alleged secret that she purports to have never told anyone else before. It really does not add up.

The secret game is merely pretense, often a prerequisite for the getting-to-know-you phase. Telling secrets, like crying, is a false vulnerability ploy. Telling improvised secrets is a game women used to get the man (you) to believe that she is being vulnerable. If her game works, you will respond by opening up yourself. You will begin to trust her with your very own secrets and she is that much closer to her goal. Another reason women tell secrets is to garner sympathy. The goal is to break through your emotional walls, learn about you and utilize her femininity to engage your sentiments.

The next time that a woman proclaims to be telling you a secret just listen. Do not respond by revealing your own secrets. No matter how many secrets she decides to reveal to you, do not reveal anything that you would not mind repeating to your grandmother. She will grow increasingly inquisitive and want to know secrets about you and will ask you about them immediately, in some cases.

When she asks you intimate details about your life and you do not give her what she wants, see if she does not try emotional blackmail. She will bring notice to all of the "secrets" that she has told you and express that she cannot believe you will not tell her whatever it is she is asking. This interrogation tactic is designed to utilize guilt and emotional peer pressure in order for you to submit to her wishes.

Head Game #3 The Unavailable Game

SO YOU HAVE MET A WOMAN that you are interested in. The only problem is that you can never seem to ever track her down. She always has something to do because she has so much going on that she has to schedule spending time with you days or weeks in advance. Even worse, she is never available on weekends and does not answer her phone past a certain "respectable" hour during the week. You can attribute this behavior to one of three things. One, she is involved with someone else; two, she is really busy with work, school, or family; or three, she is playing the unavailable game.

You will know if a woman is involved with someone else if she is always at work, in-transit or running errands when you talk to her. If she is involved with someone else, she cannot spend time with you on the weekends because her weekends are already spoken for. She cannot talk to you after a certain hour because she is with another guy. If you do happen to talk to her at night the conversation will be short, unless she is spending the night alone.

She may tell you that she is involved with someone else or she may not. It really just depends on what she wants from you and what type of guy she thinks you are. She may want you to be in her rotation or she may just want you to gradually replace her main guy (boyfriend or fiancé').

Depending on her profession, year and level in school or family situation, you may have come across someone that is genuinely busy. When dealing with someone that is extremely busy, she may initiate impromptu dinners/lunches when cancellations or changes occur in her schedule. The way you will know that she is busy and hence not playing the unavailable game is by the frequency and sincerity of her communication with you. You will also know by how much communicative access that she gives you. A woman that is busy will not mind providing work and personal email and phone numbers. However, a woman that is involved will keep certain contact information private.

Women play the unavailable game because countless books have been written that advise them to be sparingly available for men that are not committed to them. For some this game works. If you have met someone that is playing the game, do not fault her, she just does not know any better. She believes that if she is unavailable, you will want her even more. If she reads those types of books, or has spoken to her girlfriends that read those books, she intentionally will not: answer the phone every time that you call, respond to text messages immediately, or accept a date if it has not been scheduled far in advance, even if she is available for said calls, text or dining invitations.

She will always act like she is busy and try to keep conversations short when she does answer your calls. If this type of woman has caught your interest the best you can do is try to de-program her. How does one accomplish that you ask? It involves both parties being honest and truly vulnerable.

If you want a woman to reveal her schedule and stop playing the unavailable game, you may just have to reveal your own schedule first. De-programming will not be an easy task but it may be worth it in the end--only you know if it is worth the risk.

Head Game #4   Social Media

WOMEN USE SOCIAL MEDIA outlets as a spy tool. If there are some things you would rather keep private never give a woman that you are romantically interested in access to your social networks, period! There are exceptions to every rule but finding one here would be akin to finding a needle in the proverbial haystack. The only reason a woman wants access to a potential suitors social network is to size up the competition. Women do not care what your hobbies and interest are or whether you have photos of your family reunion posted. The only thing they want to know is how many other women post to your page, have pictures on your page, like and/or comment on your photos etc.

If you start dating a woman and she asks you to add her on any of your social networks, trust and believe it is for her to stake her claim on you. You may have only been out with her a few times but if she is allowed the opportunity, she will blatantly or subtly broadcast to the entire network that you are associated with her in some way.

Here's how it works. The first thing that she will check for is if you have any friends/followers in common. Next she will begin to post anecdotes about the time that the two of you spend together. She will not use your name initially but she will leave clues in order for any other female detectives that have access to your social network to know that she has been with you. For instance, if you post something like "Hanging out at X Restaurant" she will post "Had a fabulous meal at X Restaurant and an even better night (wink)." It will not take long for the network to put one and one together.

If you do not put an end to her posting anecdotes she will soon get comfortable doing it with more frequency. Eventually she will begin posting messages about how she "misses you," is "looking forward to seeing you" etc. Before you know what hit you, she will be demanding that you let the world (the network) know that you are with her by changing your status to "in a relationship with HER" or directly tagging you in pictures.

These spy tools can be used by anyone on your network. Women will have girlfriends or family members add you to their networks just so that they can keep track of you. They do not stop there either. Women will actually send you inbox messages from a friend or family member's account posing as the friend or family member. Yes! They do this frequently.

Take my advice…do not give women you are romantically or sexually involved with access to your social networks…unless you are serious.

Head Game #5 Just Friends

THIS GAME CAN BE PLAYED from the onset or even after you get the Panties. From the beginning, women may profess they are not really looking for anything serious. This is all a part of the getting-to-know-you pretense. Women typically do not want to scare men away by saying they are ready to be married and have children on the first date.

When a woman meets an attractive guy (physically or financially), wedding bells go off and they fantasize about where the ceremony will be (See *Bridget Jones Diary* for a great example). They know if they tell men this, it would only scare them away. So what do they do instead? They set the "let's just be friends" trap. Do not believe those words unless her actions are in compliance.

In other words, if she tells you that she just wants to be friends but wants you to: call, take her on dates that you pay for, meet your parents, travel out of town with you, meet all of your friends etc. do not buy it! If she really means that she wants to just be friends with you, revisit the "Friends Categories" from **Rule 2** in order to understand where you fit in.

If you get the Panties, and she tells you that she just wants to be friends…still, do not believe it. Women usually play this game if they sense that you do not want anything serious. If you have hijacked the Panties by telling her what she wanted to hear initially you cannot expect that she *only* wants to be friends just because you were not sincere. Once her ego is involved she will do almost anything to get you—to get Pockets. She will say she is okay with whatever you want and hope that you stick around long enough to change your mind. Simply put, do not buy it.

Head Game #6   Sexting

Women appeal to the head below the belt to get what they want too. Sexting is one way they do it. They actually think that there is a such thing as bad Panties. They do not know that guys would take Panties from 80% of the women they come across, even the unattractive ones. Most women think that their Panties are special. They think that they can perform some magic trick with the Panties that will make you want to commit. A friend once told me though that, "you cannot fuck the love out of a man."

Women will try to lure you with the Panties and hope that you decide to stay for more. Whether women want a serious relationship to get to the Pockets, or they want to pick from several Pockets, for women Panties is only step two of the Head→Heart→Pockets process. If you are sending and receiving sex messages she may be further along in her game than you are in yours.

Head Game #7   The Ms. Nice Girl Act

Have you ever been seeing someone that started sending you motivational messages? Not every woman that sends motivational messages is playing a Head Game. A number of things have to be in-play before you know if a woman is playing this game. First, you should be in the very early stages of getting to know her. Secondly, you should consistently be getting the Panties (despite being in the early stages of getting to know her). Thirdly, she should be sending you sext messages. If those three things are in-play <u>and</u> she starts sending motivational or religious inspired messages, she is playing a Head Game. Some women play this Head Game because they are not comfortable with their own sexuality and want to give you an impression that they are "good." For these women, the last thing they want is for a man to think of them as an easy lay. Even the women that are easy lays want romance and candles and a guy that cares about them sometimes. When a woman is screwing your brains out and subsequently inviting you to church or sending motivational messages Monday morning, she is playing a Head Game.

Women will also play this Head Game to keep the lines of communication open. If she has not talked to you for the day, or several days, and she desperately wants to hear your voice she may not call and ask to see you. What she wants is for you to ask to see her. She does not want to appear like she is more interested in you than you are in her. The way to get around looking like she is chasing you is to send you a motivational message.

When you see a motivational message, most likely, you will respond. If only to say thank you, surely you will reply. When she get's your reply she takes it as an invitation for more conversation, so she gets what she wants. You think she is one of the most thoughtful people you have ever met, and she gets more of your time. Score for her.

Head Game#8   Seductive Dancing

Seductive dancing can be traced back to tribal days. Even animals do mating dancing. It is a Head Game because women use it to get men to start thinking about sex—step two in the female process. Women know that men want a lady in the streets and freak in the sheets. Although dancing seductively is not ladylike, it surely gives a man a preview of what he will get in the sheets.

Perhaps there are a few women that go to dances just to dance. If you see a woman dancing seductively she most likely is not part of that group. Women do not dance seductively just because they like to dance. Women that just like to dance do line dances, take lessons, or join dance clubs. They do not dance seductively in public. When you see a woman dancing seductively in public it is because she wants to attract some male attention. What she wants to do with that attention will vary. Rest assured that she definitely wants to be noticed.

Head Game #9 The Trust Fall

Never trust a woman that tells you "You can trust me". Trust is not like borrowing a person's cars, it does not require permission. Trusting someone is something that happens naturally over a course of time. Trust is not a tangible object so it cannot be passed around like an offering plate. Women treat trust like a joint account—each person puts a little in. Trust does not work that way though. Just as she cannot be a little pregnant; in the same vein, you cannot trust someone a little bit. You either trust someone or you do not. When you do trust someone you surely do not need his/her permission to do so.

Inviting you to trust her is a Head Game because like the other Head Games, the purpose is to get you to reveal something deeply personal about your own life. Knowing is important for women. The more they know the more ammunition they have.

Before talking to a woman you really should be read your Miranda Rights because everything you say (or do) can and will be used against you. When do you trust a woman? That depends, but certainly not when she asks you to.

Canise Gray

Heart: Women Create Their Own Relationships

YOU TAKE THE LEAD, she chooses the destination. Women are literal creatures so long as it benefits them. When it comes to getting something they want the glass is always half-full. Women create their own relationships with your assistance. For every inch you give she will take a mile. You say you are not ready to be in a relationship now. While you think that statement absolves you of all liability and you are free to "just have fun" she has zeroed in on the operative word "now." Now is a very dicey word so let's use it in a context that you understand.

If you want to have sex with a woman and she tells you "I do not want to have sex right now," what does it mean? In this situation you will interpret *now* to mean not at that particular time. But, you will probably think that at some point in the future she *will* want to have sex. Not only will she want to have sex, you will surmise that she will want to and will in fact have sex with *you*.

In another context now means not now and not ever. Now is the politically correct way to say no. Have you ever applied for a job and received a rejection letter? Before you even open the envelope or email you already know that the words therein, no matter how nice or subtly put mean "NO." When you open the message that reads, "...we do not have an opening now, but will keep your resume on file," you count it a loss and move on. You do not go to the job every day without pay working your ass off in hopes that someone will see what great work you are doing and decide to pay you. Because in this context you know that *now* means "no."

When you tell a woman, "I do not want to be in a relationship right now," you are likely using *now* in the context of NO or translated to mean "I do not want you."

This is a concept that women do not grasp. In a relationship context *now* always has the "maybe later" meaning for a woman.

For a woman *now* is interpreted literally and thus means:
- At the present
- At the moment
- At this time
- Currently
- At this instant
- At this point

And, even if she never admits it, *now* is always followed by an unspoken:
- But later
- But when I'm ready
- But I'm moving towards
- But I'm really thinking about…

So when you tell a woman "I'm not looking/ready for a relationship," in your language you are saying,

"You look good enough to have some fun with but I do not want a relationship with **you**."

But, you know that if you say exactly what you mean you may not get what you want. So you speak in your own language in order to still get the Panties and you say something like "I'm not looking/ready for a relationship right now."

Because men and women do not speak the same language, when you say that she hears:

"At this moment/point I'm not ready for a relationship; but I am really thinking about moving towards having a relationship later with you."

If you want to avoid your intentions being lost in translation you will have to speak her language. You have to say exactly what you mean. Replace the "now" with "with you" and she will get it.

Women speak sign language. Whether you know it or not your actions will validate whatever relationship a woman has created in her mind. Every single thing you do is a "sign" that reiterates her interpretation of "now" to mean "but later" is correct. How does it happen? When you open your mouth to say you are not ready for a relationship *now* there is an episode of Charlie Brown playing in the background and all she hears is "womp woomp wooooomp woomp woomp womp."

If you meet her friends and family look out! Even if you have said you are not looking for a relationship if you meet a woman's friends and family be careful! Why? Remember it is not about what you say or how many times you say it. What you say does not matter. But, what friends and family members say does matter. What they say and what you do validate her belief that she is in a relationship with you. Going to a family function tells her that you care about, that you want to be with her, that she is special.

Pockets & Panties

Think back to the last time you met a woman's friends or family. Do you remember hearing, "I've heard so much about you?" Of course you do! Those words are not to be taken lightly. They *have* heard a lot about you. They heard so much about you that they started pressuring her to bring you around. When introductions are made you may really be meeting folks for the first time but they really are just putting a face with the name as it relates to you.

By the time you meet friends and family a woman has told so many things about you and the "relationship" because she needs validation. She needs someone else to tell her all the sign language she has been reading is accurate. That is what friends and family do for her. Friends and family listen to how wonderful you are, and how much you have going for yourself, and how perfect the two of you are together. Talking to friends and family about the relationship is a double edge sword though because eventually they start to question her about where you are.

After she has created the perfect relationship in her mind, and the minds of her friends and family, everyone will want to know why you are not with her at the birthday parties, holidays and the like. This turns into pressure from her to have you show up. She will start inviting you to everything under the sun, even things she has no real desire to attend, just so that everyone she has been talking to about you can finally meet you. Whether it is a holiday party, family dinner or cocktail hour when you are invited to an event its more about her ego and the need to validate the relationship she has created than it is you attending the event.

She wants to be seen with you in public because she created a relationship. When you acquiesce she interprets it as sign language that you are closer to being ready for the relationship she has already created. Her friends and family know where you work, where you live, what type of furniture you have. They have already told her how perfect the two of you are together and that you make a cute couple.

The day she met you she told someone about you. The day you called her she told even more people about you. Once the two of you had a date, whether you just hung out at her house or actually went to some public accommodation, her entire circle of girlfriends, co-workers, and close family members where told blow-by-blow all about you--her version of course. Before you went out with her she'd already had input on what dress to wear and what lip gloss to apply.

If you are a catch—financially stable and attractive mainly—or if you have potential, by the time you meet the circle of friends, she has spent weeks building you up in their minds. When that happens ego kicks into overdrive. You become something she has to have not because you are the most compatible but rather because she has told everyone about you and she does not want to have to explain a break-up before the formal introduction. She does not want to look stupid and be the only person not coupled off at group or family events—especially when everyone knows that she is with Mr. Perfect (YOU). To get everything she wants- the relationship she created, the life, the trips, house, dogs, car—she will go after your heart.

Pockets & Panties

COOKING

IF YOU HAPPEN UPON A WOMAN THAT COOKS consider yourself blessed. Women believe that the stomach is one of the quickest ways to a man's heart; thus, cooking for someone is a special kind of love. If you have a woman that does not cook then you should be worried. If a woman does not cook for you she simply does not love you. Cooking requires thinking about the wants and needs of another person. Cooking is a selfless act that requires preparation and planning. Ask any cook the best thing about a meal and s/he will tell you it is not the first or last bite of a delectable dish; rather it is the satisfaction on the faces of those for which the dish was prepared.

WOMAN THAT WILL NOT COOK
A woman that does not cook is not to be trusted. Nowadays some women act as if proclaiming that they do not cook is to be commended. Do not be fooled, it most certainly is not. Somewhere in the fight for voting rights and equal pay a chemical and social imbalance replaced rational thinking in some women. The same women that proudly proclaim they do not cook still expect a man to "be a man." That is, these women want a man that makes more money than they do. They want a man to spend his money on them paying for dates, vacations, and jewelry among other things. They want a man to take out the trash, pump the gas, fix whatever is broken, and protect them. They want a man to pay his bills along with theirs and pay for breakfast, lunch, and dinner—that they are not even willing to cook. Absolutely absurd! A woman that will not cook—not to be confused with a woman that does not know how—is a woman that I suggest you bypass.

WOMEN THAT CANNOT COOK

A woman that cannot cook should simply learn how. This is the woman that will prepare a meal that you simply do not like. Her chicken may be raw and undercooked or extra dry and lifeless. Her rice may always come out mushy and her spaghetti and meatballs may be of the canned variety but the fact that she cooks is what matters most. If you have a woman that cannot cook take her to a cooking class or strap her down and make her watch the Cooking Channel!

WOMEN THAT COOK

Women that can cook good food are as rare as a shooting star. These women will of course use their kitchen tools to carve their way into your heart. If you are accustomed to dealing with women that do not cook, this type of woman will surely score points with you. The important thing to look for with a woman that cooks is consistency. Of course she is going to cook in the beginning. She will probably make you breakfast in bed when you spend the night at her house the first time. If she is really good she will make breakfast even when she spends the night at your house. You will know her cooking skills were used just to hook you if the Sunday dinners turn into Sunday take-out. Initially she will pull out all the stops. After awhile she will get comfortable and that is when you find out if she was cooking just for you or if she really does cook…generally. If she cares about you she will continue to cook for you. In the beginning however cooking may be just another weapon in her expansive armory.

GIFTS

Even though money cannot buy love, some people think that it can. Because some women adopt this concept they will shower men with gifts in hopes to buy a relationship. The gift does not have to be anything expensive. It could be something as simple as sneaking a favorite cookie inside your briefcase, or souvenir from a recent vacation.

No matter the cost of the gift, if a woman buys or makes something "just to let you know that she was thinking about you," but has an expectation other than gratitude attached to it…be careful. Once you see that she is willing to do little things for you, you will be more inclined to reciprocate which gets her closer to the *Pockets*.

SEX

Sex, any type of sex, is the biggest weapon in a woman's arsenal. Why? Mainly because men want it so much. One friend told me that men would rather have sex than eat. Because men will do just about anything for sex women have an awful lot of power in this arena. For men it is usually all about sex. Think about it. Do you sit around fantasizing about your wedding day? Probably not. Men do not typically go to clubs, bars, lounges, or even grocery stores to find a wife. Men are visual creatures and are excited by the female physique. Hence, when men do go to these places, it usually has more to do with looking for the a good time (Panties) than looking for a wife.

Like men, woman have a sexual appetite too. What distinguishes the two is women's inability to separate emotions from sex. Men have mastered the art of having emotionally detached sexual relationships. In a number of ways it is easier for men to have wild unadulterated sex with women they do not care about instead of their wives or significant others (but that is a topic for another book). When men have sex they experience an emotional release so it is a lot easier to just get up and walk away afterwards. Women are on the receiving end of the physical act of sex and thus serve more as receptacles. Even a number of promiscuous women have a lot of sex to subconsciously fill a void and thus still become emotionally attached or emotionally depleted.

Once a woman gives herself (*Panties*), there is not anything more she can give. After giving up the Panties women will want some type of compensation and even feel entitled to compensation whether financial or emotional. The earlier and more often the *Panties* come off the more entitled they will feel.

This may all seem quite extreme. However, I am only highlighting what women tell you from the beginning. Whenever you probe a woman about sex too early (at least in her mind) you will likely hear one of the following responses:

Pockets & Panties

Response	Translation
You have to feed me.	Take me out to dinner and spend some money before you start thinking about getting these Panties.
I don't know you yet.	I haven't seen your car, your house, or know how much money you make. I need to know you will spend some money on me before you get these Panties.
I don't know you that well.	I want to give you the Panties but you will think I'm a slut if I have sex with you and I just met you...just wait a few days.
Are 't you going to take me out first?	How dare you even think about getting these Panties and you haven't spent any money on me yet.
Buy me a drink.	Spend some money on me, and my friends too, and maybe I'll think about letting you get these Panties.

Canise Gray

As crazy as it may be women think that their Panties are better than the next woman's. Women think that they can perform magic tricks with the Panties and make men fall in love. They think that if men like the Panties they will spend more money, spend more time, and eventually commit. The truth of the matter is that sex alone can never make a man commit.

If you do have sex with a woman before committing to a serious relationship, as most often is the case, she is going to create her own relationship regardless of the circumstances. If you provide consistency the relationship she creates will be much more elaborate. What is consistency? Consistency is having sex with a woman consecutively so much so that she thinks she is the only woman you are having sex with. Consistency means control so you cannot provide it unless you are willing to relinquish your control.

So how do you avoid relinquishing your control? Simple, do not let women dictate your schedule or monopolize your time. If the sex was good, once the physical act of sex is over, the clock starts ticking. The longer you stay the more emotionally attached she will become. When you do leave, be it immediately after, or hours later, the games begin. She may call or text "just to see if you are ok" or "if you made it home safely?" Do not be fooled. Her primary goal is to see you again so she will say or do anything to keep her and her Panties on your mind.

Pockets & Panties

Does this mean you are supposed to have sex with women and treat them like microwave dinners that are tossed in the garbage when you have had your full? Of course not! Karma is a bitch so I believe it is best to treat people how you would like to be treated in return. As a precautionary measure however I provide these words of wisdom so that you will know what you are getting into; which in most cases is more than you bargained for. That being said, it is important to know that when you oblige a woman's request after having sex with her sooner rather than later, the relationship she creates in her head is far more elaborate.

Canise Gray

Never believe "I Love You" the first time you hear it.

It takes several months and maybe even years before you can really get to know someone. Why? Because it takes that long for the real person to appear. You meet a person's representative initially. The representative serves as the surrogate until the real person actually comes out. So, when someone tells you that they love you within the first month or year of knowing them you cannot take it for face value.

The first time that a woman tells you she loves you, she does not really mean it. How could she when she does not even know you? The first *I love you* is not spoken after she has been with you for three years, learned your routines and patterns, met your family, or cared for you even on your worse days. The first *I love you* is spoken early when you still leave the room to pass gas. The first I love you comes in the fairy tale stages of the relationship when you still speak through your representative. She may like what she sees, or better put, what you allow her to see. But, she does not love you so please do not let your ego get the best of you.

The first person to say I love you in the relationship is doing nothing more than breaking the ice. I love you is a hurdle that any romantic relationship must jump in order to move past the fairy tale stage and get to reality. Once you hear I love you, you will be more inclined to let your guard down and allow someone into your heart.

Pockets & Panties

The first I love you is more about the listener being receptive to the professor than the true feelings of the professor. The first I love you serves as a gentle knock at the door of your heart--the person on the other side merely wants to be let in.

Just as some men say I love you merely to get what they want (*Panties*), some women will use I love you to get what they want--*Pockets*. There is not a bright line rule to alert you when a woman is using I love you as a ploy. However, the caveats will never steer you wrong. So long as you remember that *What You See Is What You Get*, your Pockets will be safe. Why? Even though the first I love you is more of an ice breaker than a true profession you will know love when you see it.

PERSONAL ASSISTANT MODE

Picking up your dry cleaning, updating your resume, and making travel arrangements are tasks that you can pay someone to do. When a woman starts, whether at your request or on her own volition, acting as your own personal assistant do not think that you have hit the jackpot. If you are not interested in having a serious relationship then the aforementioned tasks, among other things, should not be delegated to the woman you are involved with unless there is reciprocity. This may prove difficult because in many instances women will volunteer to do these types of things for you. Be it house-sitting while you are on a business trip, grocery shopping or cooking dinner because you are working late, or picking up a birthday gift for your family member when you have forgotten, if you allow a woman that you are not serious about to "errand" her way into your life you are setting yourself up for trouble.

Why? Remember that Women Create Their Own Relationships! The more you allow her to do, the deeper the commitment becomes. Even if you continuously say that you are not ready for a relationship your sign language tells her that she is the one and that all she has to do is wait until you are ready.

Errands come at a cost if you are not receptive to her romantic advances. It is easy to discount the Personal Assistant attack by telling yourself "she is just being nice." A deeper analysis of the situation will reveal that her niceties are targeted towards you. In the absence of reciprocity, anything that a woman offers to do for you must yield a greater return for her or else she will not offer. If she is not receiving financial compensation and there is no bartering involved, you can rest assured that she is interested in a romantic relationship.

WHAT DO WE DO NOW?

What do we do now? How do you answer that? What kind of question is that anyway? Before answering the question there are a few things you should know. Firstly *"What do we do know?"* is a woman's last attempt to plead for your heart. Like most things women say, you have to read between the lines to fully appreciate what it means. Translated into the language women speak *what do we do now* means:

Pockets & Panties

After I've giving you everything, including my Panties; after I've cooked or paid for a few dinners myself, after I've ran your errands or otherwise become your part-time personal assistant; after I have told all my friends and family about you; after I've created this magnificent relationship starring you, you cannot just walk out on me, you have to make it work.

What do we do now is a trick because the question will make you think that whatever comes afterwards is your decision. You decide that you "want to be just friends." You know now after reading Head Game 5 that men and women typically cannot be just friends so you are setting yourself up all over again. Women only want to be just friends with a guy they are not sexually attracted to. Once she has already taken you through the head games and heart attacks, the only thing left for her, is to be in a mutually exclusive relationship with you.

When a woman ask the infamous "What do we do now?" she wants you to restore her hope in the relationship she has already created. Any response that keeps her lingering around will of course give you the immediate benefit of maintaining the status quo, but will only ultimately postpone the inevitable if you truly have no romantic interest. If you are not romantically inclined "What do we do now?" is your last chance to leave the relationship without further damage. Cut your losses because if you are able to escape the wrath of a woman scorn consider yourself lucky.

Canise Gray

POCKETS

Many books and articles have been written that aim to teach women—or at least provide tips on—how to get money from men and how to get men to commit. A number of these books have sold millions of copies because women are seemingly obsessed with finding, luring and trapping a man. I imagine however that men are not waiting in line at books stores or scouring Audible to find guidance on how to get a woman to commit. The problem for men is not a lack of women. Quite the contrary, there are more than enough woman to go around. Because women outnumber men and have been inundated with societal and familial pressures to get married before the expiration of the infamous biological clock, women have become skilled predators at catching—and in some cases even devouring—their prey…You!

Even though I too caved under the pressure and tried to "catch" a man, it is painful to admit that women chasing men just is not natural. I dare not say normal because the in today's twisted world it has become commonplace. However, there is a natural order of things--for instance, the sun sets in the east and rises in the west, water freezes at 32 degrees Fahrenheit, and birds fly south for the winter. Just as you would be cautious or fearful if things in the natural order were disrupted with respect to these things, you should also be cautious of a woman that operates contrary to the natural order of things and chases or pursues you to get Pockets.

Pockets & Panties

There is nothing wrong with showering a woman with gifts or treating her to nice things. Relationships are serious business and should be treated as such. Hence, you should be certain, before making an investment in a relationship, that the woman is invested in you and not simply what your money, status, or last name can provide her. One way to do that is with a solid Prenup. . .

ABOUT THE AUTHOR

Canise Gray is an expert bargain shopper, smoothie maker, and brownie baker that moonlights as a "professional." She lives with her family in The District.

www.ingramcontent.com/pod-product-compliance
Lightning Source LLC
Chambersburg PA
CBHW061341040426
42444CB00011B/3031